EMMANUEL JOSEPH

Fortunes Built, Comparative Narratives of Silicon Valley and Real Estate Billionaires

Copyright © 2025 by Emmanuel Joseph

All rights reserved. No part of this publication may be reproduced, stored or transmitted in any form or by any means, electronic, mechanical, photocopying, recording, scanning, or otherwise without written permission from the publisher. It is illegal to copy this book, post it to a website, or distribute it by any other means without permission.

First edition

This book was professionally typeset on Reedsy.
Find out more at reedsy.com

Contents

1	Chapter 1: The Origins of Ambition	1
2	Chapter 2: Visionaries and Their Visions	3
3	Chapter 3: The Power of Innovation	5
4	Chapter 4: The Role of Failure	7
5	Chapter 5: Building Empires	9
6	Chapter 6: The Influence of Technology	12
7	Chapter 7: Strategic Networking	14
8	Chapter 8: Philanthropy and Social Impact	16
9	Chapter 9: Navigating Legal and Ethical Challenges	19
10	Chapter 10: The Role of Mentorship	21
11	Chapter 11: Adapting to Changing Markets	23
12	Chapter 12: Legacy and Lessons Learned	26

1

Chapter 1: The Origins of Ambition

Ambition is a seed that germinates in the fertile soil of one's upbringing, experiences, and environment. For many Silicon Valley billionaires, their origins were marked by a fascination with technology and a desire to solve complex problems. Growing up in an era where computers were becoming household items, these future tech moguls were tinkering with circuits and code while their peers played outside. Their relentless curiosity and early exposure to computing laid the foundation for a lifetime of innovation. In contrast, real estate billionaires often found their ambitions ignited by the tangible allure of property and construction. The sight of towering buildings and the realization that land could be transformed into valuable assets inspired them from a young age.

While the pathways to success in Silicon Valley and real estate are distinct, the common denominator is a drive to create something extraordinary. Silicon Valley's tech pioneers, like Steve Jobs and Bill Gates, were not just motivated by financial success but by a passion for technology and its potential to change the world. They were willing to take risks, drop out of college, and invest countless hours into developing their ideas. This fervor for innovation and the belief that technology could improve lives propelled them forward. Real estate magnates, such as Donald Trump and Sam Zell, were driven by the challenge of transforming landscapes and the strategic intricacies of property deals. Their ambition was fueled by the tangible results of their efforts—skyscrapers that pierced the sky and developments that reshaped cities.

The environments in which these individuals were raised also played a significant role in nurturing their ambitions. Silicon Valley billionaires often grew up in regions with robust tech ecosystems, surrounded by like-minded individuals who shared their passion for innovation. The culture of collaboration, mentorship, and access to venture capital in places like Palo Alto and Cupertino provided fertile ground for their ideas to flourish. On the other hand, real estate billionaires frequently hailed from urban areas where property values were on the rise. Their exposure to bustling city life and the dynamic real estate market around them sparked a keen interest in property development and investment.

Education and early career experiences further molded these ambitious individuals. Many Silicon Valley billionaires pursued degrees in computer science or engineering, honing their technical skills and gaining insights into the latest technological advancements. They often interned at tech companies or launched their startups from college dorm rooms. These formative experiences provided them with the knowledge and confidence to disrupt traditional industries. Real estate billionaires, however, typically gained practical experience through hands-on work in construction or property management. They learned the ropes by negotiating deals, overseeing projects, and understanding market trends. This practical knowledge, combined with a keen business acumen, set the stage for their future success.

Ultimately, the origins of ambition for Silicon Valley and real estate billionaires are a blend of passion, environment, and early experiences. While their paths diverge in terms of industry focus, the underlying drive to innovate, create, and succeed is a shared trait. These individuals' journeys from humble beginnings to towering achievements underscore the power of ambition as a catalyst for extraordinary success. The stories of their origins inspire future generations to pursue their passions relentlessly and to believe in the transformative potential of their dreams.

2

Chapter 2: Visionaries and Their Visions

Silicon Valley is a cradle for visionaries who dare to imagine a future vastly different from the present. These tech pioneers possess an uncanny ability to foresee the potential of emerging technologies and craft products that revolutionize the way we live and work. Steve Jobs, for instance, envisioned a world where technology was intuitive and accessible to all, leading to the creation of iconic devices like the iPhone and iPad. Elon Musk's vision of interplanetary travel and sustainable energy has driven the success of companies like SpaceX and Tesla. These visionaries are not merely dreamers; they are executors who turn their ambitious ideas into reality through relentless determination and innovation.

In the world of real estate, visionaries exhibit a similar propensity for transforming the landscape around them. Donald Bren, chairman of the Irvine Company, has played a pivotal role in shaping Southern California's urban and suburban environments. His vision for master-planned communities has created thriving, sustainable neighborhoods that offer a high quality of life. Harry Helmsley's foresight in acquiring and developing prime real estate in New York City has left an indelible mark on the city's skyline. These real estate visionaries possess an innate ability to identify undervalued properties and envision their potential, turning neglected areas into bustling hubs of activity and commerce.

What sets these visionaries apart is their capacity to look beyond the present and imagine a future that others cannot yet see. In Silicon Valley, this often involves anticipating technological trends and understanding how they will shape consumer behavior and industry standards. Tech visionaries are adept at recognizing the potential of nascent technologies, whether it's the internet, artificial intelligence, or renewable energy, and leveraging them to create groundbreaking products. Similarly, real estate visionaries have an acute understanding of market dynamics, demographic shifts, and urbanization trends. Their ability to predict and capitalize on these changes enables them to make strategic investments that yield substantial returns.

While their domains differ, the visionary mindset in both Silicon Valley and real estate is characterized by a willingness to take calculated risks. Tech entrepreneurs often invest heavily in research and development, betting on unproven technologies and enduring countless failures before achieving success. Real estate developers, on the other hand, commit significant capital to long-term projects that may take years to realize their full potential. The ability to take risks, coupled with a profound belief in their vision, drives these individuals to overcome obstacles and persevere in the face of adversity. Their stories are a testament to the power of vision and the transformative impact it can have on industries and societies.

Ultimately, the visions of Silicon Valley and real estate billionaires are not confined to their respective fields; they have a broader impact on the world. Tech innovations have democratized access to information, connected people across the globe, and created new industries and job opportunities. Real estate developments have revitalized cities, improved urban living conditions, and contributed to economic growth. The legacies of these visionaries extend far beyond their financial success, inspiring future generations to dream big and pursue their own transformative visions. Their stories remind us that the future is shaped by those who dare to imagine it and have the courage to bring it to life.

3

Chapter 3: The Power of Innovation

Innovation is the driving force behind the success of Silicon Valley billionaires. These tech entrepreneurs thrive on disrupting established markets and creating products that redefine how we live and work. The development of the internet, smartphones, and artificial intelligence are prime examples of their impact on society. Companies like Google, founded by Larry Page and Sergey Brin, revolutionized the way we search for information and connect with the world. Amazon, under the leadership of Jeff Bezos, transformed the retail landscape with its e-commerce platform and innovations in logistics and cloud computing. The relentless pursuit of innovation is a hallmark of Silicon Valley's tech giants, propelling them to the forefront of the global economy.

In the realm of real estate, innovation takes on a different but equally significant form. Real estate developers are constantly seeking new ways to enhance the value and functionality of properties. This involves employing cutting-edge construction techniques, sustainable building practices, and smart technologies to create modern, efficient, and environmentally friendly structures. Innovators like Jonathan Gray of Blackstone have pioneered new investment strategies and approaches to property management, driving growth and profitability in the real estate sector. The ability to innovate and adapt to changing market conditions is crucial for real estate moguls to stay competitive and achieve long-term success.

The power of innovation lies in its ability to solve problems and create new opportunities. In Silicon Valley, tech entrepreneurs are driven by a desire to address pressing challenges and improve the quality of life for people around the world. Innovations in healthcare technology, for example, have led to advancements in medical diagnostics, treatments, and patient care. The development of renewable energy solutions is helping to combat climate change and reduce our reliance on fossil fuels. These innovations not only generate significant economic value but also contribute to the greater good of society. Real estate innovators, similarly, are focused on creating spaces that meet the evolving needs of communities. The integration of green building practices, mixed-use developments, and affordable housing initiatives reflects their commitment to sustainable and inclusive urban growth.

Collaboration is a key component of the innovation process in both Silicon Valley and real estate. Tech companies often work closely with academic institutions, research organizations, and other industry players to drive innovation forward. Open-source projects and collaborative platforms enable the sharing of knowledge and resources, accelerating the pace of technological advancement. In the real estate sector, developers collaborate with architects, urban planners, and government agencies to design and execute projects that align with community needs and regulatory requirements. The exchange of ideas and expertise fosters a culture of continuous improvement and innovation, benefiting all stakeholders involved.

The impact of innovation extends far beyond the immediate benefits to individuals and companies. It drives economic growth, enhances competitiveness, and contributes to societal progress. The success stories of Silicon Valley and real estate billionaires underscore the transformative power of innovation and its ability to create lasting value. Their achievements inspire others to think creatively, embrace change, and pursue innovative solutions to the challenges we face. As we look to the future, the continued emphasis on innovation will be essential for addressing emerging issues and unlocking new possibilities for growth and development.

4

Chapter 4: The Role of Failure

Failure is an integral part of the journey to success for both Silicon Valley and real estate billionaires. In the tech industry, the culture of embracing failure as a learning opportunity is deeply ingrained. Entrepreneurs like Elon Musk and Jeff Bezos faced numerous setbacks and challenges on their path to success. Musk's early ventures, such as Zip2 and X.com, experienced significant hurdles before evolving into PayPal and SpaceX. Bezos' initial attempts to expand Amazon's product offerings were met with mixed results, but he persevered and continued to innovate. The willingness to take risks, learn from failures, and iterate on ideas is a defining characteristic of Silicon Valley's tech pioneers.

In the world of real estate, failure can be equally daunting and consequential. Economic downturns, market fluctuations, and unforeseen challenges can lead to significant financial losses and project delays. Real estate moguls like Donald Trump and Sam Zell have experienced their share of setbacks, from property value declines to legal disputes. However, their ability to navigate these challenges and emerge stronger is a testament to their resilience and adaptability. The real estate industry requires a keen understanding of market dynamics and the ability to make informed decisions in the face of uncertainty. Failure serves as a valuable teacher, providing insights that guide future strategies and investments.

One of the key lessons learned from failure is the importance of resilience.

Silicon Valley entrepreneurs often view failure as a stepping stone to success, using it as an opportunity to refine their ideas and approaches. The iterative process of developing and testing products allows for continuous improvement and innovation. This mindset encourages a culture of experimentation and risk-taking, where failure is not feared but embraced as part of the growth journey. In real estate, resilience is demonstrated through the ability to adapt to changing market conditions and pivot strategies when necessary. The capacity to weather downturns and capitalize on opportunities during recovery periods is a hallmark of successful real estate developers.

Failure also highlights the significance of perseverance and determination. The stories of Silicon Valley and real estate billionaires are filled with moments of doubt and adversity. Yet, their unwavering commitment to their goals and visions propels them forward. Tech entrepreneurs like Steve Jobs, who was ousted from Apple before making a triumphant return, exemplify the power of perseverance. Real estate moguls like Harry Helmsley, who faced numerous challenges in building his empire, showcase the importance of staying the course despite setbacks. Their journeys underscore the idea that success is not a linear path but a series of ups and downs that require grit and tenacity.

Ultimately, failure is a crucial element in the narrative of success for Silicon Valley and real estate billionaires. It shapes their character, informs their strategies, and drives their innovation. The ability to learn from mistakes, adapt to changing circumstances, and persevere in the face of adversity sets these individuals apart. Their stories serve as a reminder that failure is not the end but a necessary step on the road to achieving greatness. By embracing failure and viewing it as a valuable learning experience, future generations can build on the legacy of these billionaires and continue to push the boundaries of what is possible.

5

Chapter 5: Building Empires

The process of building empires in Silicon Valley and real estate is a testament to the power of vision, strategy, and execution. Tech billionaires create empires by developing products and services that become indispensable to consumers worldwide. Companies like Apple, Google, and Facebook have redefined industries and transformed the way we live, work, and communicate. Apple's ecosystem of devices and services, Google's dominance in search and advertising, and Facebook's social networking platform have become integral parts of daily life. The ability to anticipate consumer needs, innovate continuously, and scale rapidly are key factors in building these tech empires.

Real estate billionaires build their empires through strategic acquisitions, development projects, and property management. They identify prime locations, negotiate favorable deals, and oversee the construction of iconic structures. The Trump Organization, led by Donald Trump, has developed numerous high-profile properties, including hotels, office buildings, and golf courses. The company's ability to leverage branding and strategic partnerships has contributed to its success. Similarly, Sam Zell's Equity Group Investments has acquired and managed a diverse portfolio of real estate assets, generating significant returns for investors. The combination of strategic vision and operational excellence is key to building real estate empires.

One of the critical factors in building empires is the ability to scale operations effectively. Silicon Valley tech companies excel at scaling their products and services to reach a global audience. The network effects created by platforms like Facebook and LinkedIn enhance their value as more users join, creating a self-reinforcing cycle of growth. Tech companies invest in infrastructure, data centers, and distribution networks to support their expanding user base. In real estate, scaling involves acquiring additional properties, expanding into new markets, and optimizing property management processes. The ability to scale efficiently allows real estate developers to increase their asset base and revenue streams.

Strategic planning and execution are paramount in building empires. Tech entrepreneurs meticulously plan product launches, marketing campaigns, and international expansions. They analyze market trends, consumer behavior, and competitive landscapes to make informed decisions. Real estate developers engage in detailed market research, feasibility studies, and financial modeling to assess the viability of projects. They work closely with architects, contractors, and financiers to ensure successful project completion. The stories of successful empire builders highlight the importance of careful planning, strategic thinking, and flawless execution in achieving long-term success.

The process of building empires is also marked by a relentless pursuit of excellence. Silicon Valley billionaires continuously innovate and improve their products to stay ahead of the competition. Companies like Apple and Tesla invest heavily in research and development to introduce new features and technologies. Real estate moguls strive for excellence in design, construction, and property management. They seek to create aesthetically pleasing and functional spaces that meet the needs of tenants and residents. The commitment to excellence and the pursuit of continuous improvement are defining traits of successful empire builders.

Finally, the legacies of these empire builders extend beyond their financial achievements. Silicon Valley tech companies have transformed industries, created millions of jobs, and contributed to economic growth. Their innovations have improved the quality of life for people around the world.

CHAPTER 5: BUILDING EMPIRES

Real estate developers have shaped the skylines of cities, revitalized urban areas, and provided housing and commercial spaces for communities. The impact of their work is visible in the physical and digital landscapes they have created. The stories of these billionaires serve as an inspiration to future generations, demonstrating the power of vision, innovation, and strategic execution in building lasting empires.

6

Chapter 6: The Influence of Technology

Technology is the driving force behind the success of Silicon Valley billionaires. Innovations in software, hardware, and artificial intelligence have revolutionized industries and created new opportunities for wealth creation. The development of the internet, for example, has transformed the way we communicate, access information, and conduct business. Companies like Google and Facebook have built their empires on the foundation of digital advertising, leveraging data and analytics to deliver targeted marketing campaigns. The rise of e-commerce platforms like Amazon has reshaped the retail landscape, offering convenience and a wide range of products to consumers worldwide.

Real estate billionaires also harness technology to enhance their portfolios and improve operational efficiency. The adoption of smart building technologies allows property owners to monitor and optimize energy usage, security systems, and maintenance processes. Innovations in construction technology, such as modular building techniques and 3D printing, enable faster and more cost-effective development projects. Data-driven decision-making and predictive analytics help real estate developers identify emerging market trends, assess property values, and make informed investment choices. The integration of technology in real estate operations drives efficiency, reduces costs, and enhances the value of properties.

The influence of technology extends beyond operational efficiency to

CHAPTER 6: THE INFLUENCE OF TECHNOLOGY

impact the overall experience of tenants and residents. In Silicon Valley, tech companies prioritize user experience, developing intuitive and user-friendly interfaces that enhance customer satisfaction. Real estate developers similarly focus on creating smart, connected environments that improve the quality of life for occupants. Smart home technologies, for example, allow residents to control lighting, temperature, and security systems remotely. The use of technology in property management platforms streamlines communication between tenants and property managers, facilitating efficient issue resolution and service requests.

Collaboration between tech companies and real estate developers is becoming increasingly common, leading to innovative solutions that benefit both industries. Tech giants like Google and Amazon are investing in real estate projects to create integrated, tech-enabled communities. These developments incorporate cutting-edge technologies, green building practices, and sustainable design principles. The partnership between technology and real estate results in the creation of smart cities that offer enhanced connectivity, convenience, and sustainability. The synergy between these industries drives economic growth and improves the overall urban living experience.

The stories of Silicon Valley and real estate billionaires highlight the transformative power of technology in shaping industries and creating wealth. Their ability to leverage technological advancements and stay ahead of the curve is a key factor in their success. The continuous evolution of technology presents new opportunities and challenges, requiring these billionaires to remain agile and adaptable. As we look to the future, the influence of technology will continue to play a pivotal role in driving innovation, enhancing operational efficiency, and creating value in both the tech and real estate sectors.

7

Chapter 7: Strategic Networking

Networking is a vital component of the success of Silicon Valley and real estate billionaires. In the tech industry, connections with venture capitalists, engineers, and industry leaders are crucial for securing funding, talent, and partnerships. Silicon Valley's collaborative ecosystem fosters a culture of networking, where entrepreneurs, investors, and innovators come together to exchange ideas and resources. Events like TechCrunch Disrupt and Y Combinator Demo Day provide platforms for startups to showcase their products and attract investment. The ability to build and leverage a strong network of contacts is essential for tech entrepreneurs to navigate the competitive landscape and achieve success.

Real estate developers also rely on strategic networking to navigate the complexities of the industry. Building relationships with investors, architects, contractors, and government officials is critical for securing funding, obtaining permits, and ensuring successful project execution. Real estate moguls attend industry conferences, trade shows, and networking events to connect with potential partners and collaborators. The ability to cultivate and maintain relationships with key stakeholders enables developers to identify new opportunities, negotiate favorable deals, and navigate regulatory challenges. Strategic networking is a cornerstone of the real estate industry, facilitating growth and success.

One of the key benefits of networking is access to valuable insights and

CHAPTER 7: STRATEGIC NETWORKING

knowledge. In Silicon Valley, tech entrepreneurs often seek mentorship from experienced industry veterans who provide guidance and support. Mentorship relationships help startups navigate the early stages of development, avoid common pitfalls, and refine their business strategies. Real estate developers similarly benefit from mentorship, learning from the experiences of seasoned professionals who have successfully navigated the industry's challenges. The exchange of knowledge and expertise within a network fosters a culture of continuous learning and improvement, driving innovation and growth.

Networking also plays a crucial role in fostering collaboration and partnerships. In the tech industry, partnerships between startups and established companies can lead to strategic synergies and market expansion. Collaborations with academic institutions and research organizations drive technological advancements and innovation. Real estate developers often partner with financial institutions, construction firms, and marketing agencies to execute large-scale projects. Joint ventures and partnerships enable developers to pool resources, share risks, and achieve common goals. The ability to collaborate effectively within a network enhances the overall success of both tech entrepreneurs and real estate developers.

Ultimately, the power of networking lies in its ability to create opportunities and drive success. The stories of Silicon Valley and real estate billionaires underscore the importance of building and maintaining strong networks of contacts and collaborators. Their ability to leverage these networks for mutual benefit is a key factor in their achievements. By cultivating meaningful relationships and engaging in strategic networking, these billionaires create a supportive ecosystem that fosters innovation, growth, and long-term success. Their experiences highlight the value of networking as a critical tool for navigating the complexities of their respective industries and achieving extraordinary success.

8

Chapter 8: Philanthropy and Social Impact

Philanthropy is a significant aspect of the lives of many Silicon Valley and real estate billionaires. Driven by a desire to give back to society and address pressing global challenges, these individuals channel their wealth toward philanthropic endeavors. Tech titans like Bill Gates and Mark Zuckerberg have established foundations that focus on healthcare, education, and poverty alleviation. The Bill & Melinda Gates Foundation, for example, has made substantial contributions to global health initiatives, including efforts to combat diseases like malaria and polio. The Chan Zuckerberg Initiative aims to advance human potential and promote equal opportunity through investments in science, education, and community development.

Real estate billionaires also engage in philanthropy, using their resources to support community development and cultural initiatives. Developers like Stephen Ross and the late Eli Broad have made significant contributions to the arts, education, and public spaces. Ross's philanthropic efforts include donations to the University of Michigan and support for various community programs. Broad's contributions to the arts have left a lasting impact on cultural institutions in Los Angeles, including the establishment of The Broad museum. Real estate moguls recognize the importance of giving back to the

CHAPTER 8: PHILANTHROPY AND SOCIAL IMPACT

communities that have supported their success and strive to make a positive difference.

Philanthropy allows billionaires to address social and environmental issues that align with their values and passions. In Silicon Valley, tech entrepreneurs often focus on leveraging technology to drive social impact. Initiatives like the Giving Pledge, co-founded by Bill Gates and Warren Buffett, encourage billionaires to commit the majority of their wealth to philanthropic causes. The use of technology in philanthropy enables more effective and scalable solutions to global challenges. Real estate developers, Real estate developers, similarly, contribute to social impact by supporting affordable housing initiatives, community revitalization projects, and environmental sustainability efforts. Philanthropy provides them with an opportunity to address issues such as homelessness, urban decay, and climate change. By investing in green building practices and sustainable developments, real estate moguls contribute to environmental conservation and create healthier living spaces. Their philanthropic efforts reflect a commitment to social responsibility and a desire to create positive change in the communities they serve.

Philanthropy also serves as a means for billionaires to leave a lasting legacy. Silicon Valley entrepreneurs often focus on transformative initiatives that have the potential to make a significant and enduring impact. The work of the Gates Foundation in global health and education, for instance, aims to address systemic issues and create sustainable solutions. Real estate developers, on the other hand, leave a tangible legacy through their contributions to the built environment. The buildings and public spaces they create serve as lasting reminders of their commitment to improving urban life. Their philanthropic efforts ensure that their wealth is used to benefit future generations and address pressing societal challenges.

Moreover, philanthropy allows billionaires to align their resources with their personal values and passions. Many Silicon Valley entrepreneurs are motivated by a belief in the power of technology to drive social change. Their philanthropic initiatives often focus on leveraging innovation to address issues such as digital divide, access to education, and healthcare disparities. Real estate developers, meanwhile, are driven by a desire to create inclusive and vibrant communities. Their philanthropic efforts support initiatives that enhance urban living, promote cultural enrichment, and provide opportunities for economic development. By aligning their wealth with their values, billionaires create a positive impact that resonates with their vision for a better world.

The stories of Silicon Valley and real estate billionaires underscore the importance of philanthropy as an integral part of their journeys. Their contributions extend beyond financial success to encompass a commitment to social responsibility and community well-being. By using their resources to address pressing challenges and create positive change, these billionaires inspire others to engage in philanthropy and contribute to the greater good. Their philanthropic efforts serve as a testament to the potential of wealth to drive meaningful and lasting impact.

9

Chapter 9: Navigating Legal and Ethical Challenges

The pursuit of wealth is not without its legal and ethical challenges. Silicon Valley billionaires often face scrutiny over issues such as data privacy, monopolistic practices, and labor conditions. The rapid growth of tech companies can outpace regulatory frameworks, leading to complex legal battles and public controversies. Companies like Facebook and Google have been investigated for antitrust violations and data privacy breaches, highlighting the need for robust regulatory oversight. Navigating these challenges requires tech entrepreneurs to balance innovation with ethical responsibility and compliance with legal standards.

In the real estate industry, legal and ethical challenges can arise from zoning laws, environmental regulations, and community opposition. Real estate developers must navigate a complex web of regulations and approvals to bring their projects to fruition. Issues such as gentrification and displacement of communities can lead to ethical dilemmas and public backlash. Developers like Stephen Ross and Donald Trump have faced legal disputes and controversies related to their projects, underscoring the importance of ethical decision-making and transparency. Addressing these challenges requires a commitment to ethical practices, community engagement, and compliance with legal requirements.

One of the key challenges in both industries is maintaining transparency and accountability. Silicon Valley companies often operate in a fast-paced and highly competitive environment, where the pressure to innovate and deliver results can lead to ethical lapses. The stories of tech giants like Uber and Theranos highlight the consequences of ethical failings and the importance of corporate governance. Real estate developers, similarly, must ensure transparency in their dealings with investors, tenants, and communities. Ethical practices and open communication are essential for building trust and maintaining a positive reputation.

Navigating legal and ethical challenges also requires a proactive approach to risk management. Tech entrepreneurs must stay abreast of evolving regulatory landscapes and implement robust data protection and compliance measures. Real estate developers must conduct thorough due diligence and engage in responsible development practices. The ability to anticipate and mitigate risks is crucial for long-term success in both industries. By adopting a proactive and ethical approach, billionaires can navigate challenges effectively and uphold their commitment to responsible business practices.

Ultimately, the stories of Silicon Valley and real estate billionaires highlight the importance of ethical leadership and legal compliance in the pursuit of wealth. Their experiences underscore the need for a balanced approach that prioritizes innovation and growth while adhering to ethical principles and legal standards. By navigating these challenges with integrity and responsibility, billionaires can achieve sustainable success and contribute positively to society. Their journeys serve as a reminder that ethical leadership is essential for building lasting and impactful legacies.

10

Chapter 10: The Role of Mentorship

Mentorship plays a crucial role in shaping the trajectories of Silicon Valley and real estate billionaires. Tech entrepreneurs often find guidance and support from experienced industry veterans who provide valuable insights and advice. The mentor-mentee relationship fosters growth and innovation, helping startups navigate the challenges of early-stage development. Silicon Valley's culture of mentorship is exemplified by programs like Y Combinator, where seasoned entrepreneurs mentor and invest in promising startups. The support and guidance provided by mentors enable tech entrepreneurs to refine their ideas, avoid common pitfalls, and accelerate their growth.

In the real estate industry, mentorship helps aspiring developers navigate the complexities of the market and build successful careers. Seasoned moguls like Sam Zell and Stephen Ross have mentored numerous young developers, sharing their experiences and expertise. Mentorship relationships in real estate often involve hands-on learning and practical guidance, helping mentees develop the skills and knowledge needed to succeed. The mentor's insights into market trends, negotiation strategies, and project management are invaluable for aspiring developers. The legacy of mentorship extends beyond individual success, contributing to the overall advancement of the real estate industry.

One of the key benefits of mentorship is the transfer of knowledge and experience. In Silicon Valley, mentors provide insights into industry trends, technological advancements, and business strategies. Their guidance helps startups navigate the competitive landscape and make informed decisions. Real estate mentors share their expertise in areas such as property acquisition, development financing, and regulatory compliance. The exchange of knowledge and experience within a mentorship relationship fosters a culture of continuous learning and improvement. The mentor's wisdom and experience serve as a valuable resource for mentees, helping them achieve their goals and aspirations.

Mentorship also provides emotional support and encouragement. The journey to success is often filled with challenges, setbacks, and moments of doubt. Having a mentor who believes in their potential and provides encouragement can make a significant difference for entrepreneurs and developers. The mentor's support and guidance help mentees stay motivated, build confidence, and persevere through difficult times. The stories of successful Silicon Valley and real estate billionaires often include the influence of mentors who played a pivotal role in their journeys. The mentor-mentee relationship is built on trust, respect, and mutual support, creating a positive and nurturing environment for growth.

Ultimately, mentorship is a powerful tool for fostering success and innovation in both Silicon Valley and real estate. The stories of billionaires in these industries highlight the transformative impact of mentorship on their careers and achievements. By providing guidance, sharing knowledge, and offering support, mentors help shape the next generation of entrepreneurs and developers. The legacy of mentorship is evident in the continued growth and advancement of these industries. The experiences of Silicon Valley and real estate billionaires serve as a reminder of the importance of mentorship in achieving extraordinary success.

11

Chapter 11: Adapting to Changing Markets

The ability to adapt to changing market dynamics is a common trait among billionaires in both Silicon Valley and real estate. Tech entrepreneurs must stay ahead of technological trends and evolving consumer preferences. The rapid pace of technological advancements requires continuous innovation and agility. Companies like Apple, Google, and Amazon have demonstrated the ability to pivot and innovate in response to changing market conditions. Apple's transition from personal computers to mobile devices, Google's expansion into cloud computing, and Amazon's diversification into various industries are examples of successful adaptation. The ability to anticipate and respond to market shifts is essential for sustained success in the tech industry.

In the real estate sector, developers must navigate economic cycles, demographic shifts, and urbanization trends. The ability to adapt to these changes is crucial for identifying new opportunities and mitigating risks. Real estate moguls like Sam Zell and Stephen Ross have successfully navigated multiple economic downturns by adjusting their strategies and diversifying their portfolios. Zell's focus on distressed assets during market downturns and Ross's investment in mixed-use developments are examples of adaptive strategies. Real estate developers must stay informed about market trends, conduct thorough research, and make data-driven decisions to remain competitive and achieve long-term success.

Adaptation also involves embracing new technologies and methodologies. In Silicon Valley, tech entrepreneurs continuously explore emerging technologies such as artificial intelligence, blockchain, and quantum computing. The willingness to invest in research and development and experiment with new ideas is a hallmark of successful tech companies. Real estate developers are increasingly incorporating smart building technologies, sustainable design practices, and data analytics into their projects. The integration of technology in property development and management enhances efficiency, reduces costs, and improves the overall value of properties. The ability to leverage technology and innovate within their respective fields is a key factor in the success of both tech entrepreneurs and real estate developers.

One of the critical aspects of adaptation is the ability to make informed and timely decisions. In Silicon Valley, tech entrepreneurs must assess market trends, consumer behavior, and competitive landscapes to make strategic decisions. The rapid pace of technological change requires a proactive approach to decision-making and the ability to pivot quickly. Real estate developers must conduct thorough due diligence, assess market conditions, and evaluate investment opportunities. The ability to make data-driven decisions and adjust strategies in response to changing market dynamics is essential for achieving success. The stories of Silicon Valley and real estate billionaires highlight the importance of agility and foresight in navigating evolving markets.

Ultimately, the ability to adapt to changing markets requires a mindset that embraces flexibility and innovation. Silicon Valley entrepreneurs understand the importance of remaining agile and responsive to new developments. They continuously explore new technologies, engage with emerging trends, and refine their business models to stay competitive. Real estate developers, similarly, must be proactive in identifying and capitalizing on market opportunities. The ability to pivot and make strategic decisions in response to market shifts ensures their long-term success.

The stories of Silicon Valley and real estate billionaires highlight the

CHAPTER 11: ADAPTING TO CHANGING MARKETS

importance of a forward-thinking approach. Their success is rooted in their capacity to anticipate and respond to changes in the market landscape. Whether it involves adopting new technologies, exploring untapped markets, or adjusting investment strategies, their ability to adapt is a key factor in their achievements. By embracing change and continuously innovating, these billionaires create value and drive growth in their respective industries. Their experiences serve as a testament to the importance of adaptability and foresight in achieving extraordinary success.

12

Chapter 12: Legacy and Lessons Learned

As Silicon Valley and real estate billionaires reach the zenith of their success, they reflect on their legacies and the lessons learned along their journeys. Tech visionaries ponder the lasting impact of their innovations on society and the world. Companies like Apple, Google, and Amazon have left an indelible mark on the digital age, shaping how we live, work, and communicate. The innovations introduced by these tech giants continue to influence industries and improve the quality of life for people worldwide. Real estate moguls, on the other hand, leave behind tangible legacies in the form of iconic structures and transformed urban landscapes. Their developments have revitalized cities, created job opportunities, and contributed to economic growth.

One of the key lessons learned by these billionaires is the importance of resilience and perseverance. The journeys of Silicon Valley and real estate billionaires are marked by challenges, failures, and setbacks. Their ability to overcome adversity and stay committed to their visions is a defining characteristic of their success. The stories of entrepreneurs like Steve Jobs, Elon Musk, Donald Trump, and Sam Zell underscore the value of persistence and determination. These individuals demonstrate that success is not achieved overnight but through continuous effort, learning, and adaptation.

Another important lesson is the significance of ethical leadership and social responsibility. The impact of Silicon Valley and real estate billionaires

CHAPTER 12: LEGACY AND LESSONS LEARNED

extends beyond their financial achievements to encompass a commitment to improving society. Their philanthropic endeavors, innovative solutions, and community-focused initiatives reflect a dedication to making a positive difference. By prioritizing ethical practices, transparency, and social impact, these billionaires set an example for future generations. Their legacies serve as a reminder that true success involves not only personal gain but also contributing to the greater good.

The stories of Silicon Valley and real estate billionaires also highlight the value of mentorship and collaboration. The guidance and support provided by mentors have played a crucial role in shaping their journeys. Collaboration with partners, investors, and industry experts has enabled them to achieve remarkable results. The experiences of these billionaires emphasize the importance of building strong networks, seeking advice, and working together to achieve common goals. By fostering a culture of mentorship and collaboration, future entrepreneurs and developers can continue to drive innovation and success.

Ultimately, the legacies of Silicon Valley and real estate billionaires are defined by their contributions to the world. Their innovations, developments, and philanthropic efforts have created lasting value and transformed industries. The lessons learned from their journeys serve as valuable guides for aspiring billionaires, emphasizing the importance of ambition, resilience, ethical leadership, and collaboration. Their stories inspire future generations to pursue their passions, embrace challenges, and strive for greatness. The impact of their work will continue to shape the world for years to come, leaving a legacy of innovation, growth, and positive change.

Fortunes Built: Comparative Narratives of Silicon Valley and Real Estate Billionaires delves into the fascinating journeys of some of the world's most successful entrepreneurs. This book presents a comparative analysis of the contrasting yet equally compelling paths of Silicon Valley tech titans and real estate moguls. Through twelve engaging chapters, readers will explore the origins, ambitions, and visions that propelled these billionaires to extraordinary heights.

From the innovative minds driving technological advancements in Silicon

Valley to the strategic masterminds reshaping urban landscapes, this book uncovers the power of vision, resilience, and strategic networking. Each chapter offers insights into the unique challenges and triumphs faced by these industry leaders, highlighting the importance of innovation, adaptability, and ethical leadership.

Readers will discover the pivotal role of failure in shaping success, the influence of mentorship, and the profound impact of philanthropy on society. Through vivid narratives and real-world examples, **Fortunes Built** provides a comprehensive understanding of the factors that contribute to building empires in both the tech and real estate sectors.

Whether you are an aspiring entrepreneur, a business enthusiast, or simply curious about the stories behind immense wealth, **Fortunes Built** offers valuable lessons and inspiration from the lives of those who have shaped our modern world. Join us on this captivating journey to uncover the secrets behind the fortunes built by Silicon Valley and real estate billionaires.